The Net
& other poems

Victor di Suvero

Pennywhistle Press
Malibu & San Francisco | 1987

ISBN 0-938631-01-2
Library of Congress Catalog Card Number 86-060725
Cover photographs by Barbara Windom
Designed by John McBride
Composition at *turnaround* (Berkeley)
Printed in the United States of America

This book is dedicated to

BARBARA

*and to that community of friends whose
spirit and love have helped to shape these poems,
with appreciation.*

THE NET POEMS: *The Question of Net, Consider It, The Net Regarded, Sing Song, The Net Now, The Net as Light, & The Net Folded* [7], Talking about Sea [12], Questions [13], Pedro Point from Stinson Beach [14], Praises [15], Saturday Morning [16], Three Songs [17], Declaration [20], Recognition [21], The Shadow Dance [21], Spaceborne [22], Varda Poem [23], Day on the Bay [23], Address to the Singer [24], For Toni [25], For the Person Who Sounds the Future [26], For Love That's Given [27], Henrietta [28], Steel Striding [29], Go Daughter of Mine [30], For the Marriage of Romana & Nico [31], That Which Is [32], Progress [33], It Did Not Start Hesitantly [34], Corollary [35], Garland [36], The Grey Heron in the Garden [44], Into the Air [45], Harmony [46], Every Thing [47], The Promised Land [48], Prismatic Function [49], Eight Views of the World [50], Invocation [54], Gauguin's Self Portrait [55], Road Poem [56], Alarms [57], Measure [57], Stuff [58], Not Dream [61], There are Certain Goodbyes [62], Farewell to the House of These Years.

THE NET

The Question of Net

Where do we begin?
With Abraham?
Or further back –
At the beginning?

Do I tell my children
That because of the Inquisition
An ancestor left Malaga
For Padua and Venice –
Some say by ship,
Others say on foot up the coast –
And then across the mountains
Always across the mountains,
And across the sea.

Is that the beginning
Of this net?

It always starts
With just a piece of string
A cord to tie us in
To let us go,
To be, and

There are moments
When we are not the knots,
But the spaces in between
For which there is no name
But which is light.

We know our end
But how do we begin?

Consider It

Consider now
This net we knot.

Well versed, our hands turn twine
Into a fabric that will catch fish
To feed us in the feast.

Snare and protection when wrapped round
The gladiator's arm
It becomes a veil before the Altar.

Drawn taut it becomes a grid
Which is the cry of order.

Thrown down into a pile
It invents complexities.

It is the racetrack of the blood
Sustenance of spies, rune of circumstance
And prime connection between banks.

Connection and division
Analog of life
Each knot a moment caught,
Fixing a new dimension to the rest.
We see through it, catch with it
Or are caught in it ourselves.

It is that by which the flesh is trapped.

It is also that through which the spirit leaves.

This net.

The Net Regarded

There is that part of me that feels
"I am not worthy" no matter
How small the comfort or the space.

There is that other part that knows
How short the time between the sun's rise and set
And that nothing is enough.

Between the two there is the weaving of a net
Which catches things that help;
Some furred, some feathered,
Some smooth and sweet,
Some full of smoke, dry and pungent,
Others made of dreams,
Each of which becomes
Another part of me.

Sing Song

As the day is done
I am the needle's point
Weaving the net again
Where it was torn.

I am the net made whole again
And the boat's bilge in which I lie.

I am cast into the swirling sea at dawn
And become the water's shape
To fold the dark where it was light.

I am the fish come home again
And the sky's depth in which I fly.

The Net Now

I have become the net
Indistinguishable from any debt I owe.
The calls I make each day
Are all the strands I weave
To keep it strung together.

The produce of the mine unmined,
The school of fish still free to swim,
The one great gem still in the ground.

I count each foot of twine,
Each float, each piece of rope.
I lay it gently in the hold.
I play with it to keep it light.
I sleep on it and dream of it
And end up so caught in it
That I become the harvest
And the mine,
And it is the net itself
That ends up eating me
And mine.

Each dawn I wake
I see my children shake in it,
My parents bones are in it,
My vertigo, my hopes
And all my world is in it now
Knowing
I must cast it out again
To bring it home.

The Net as Light

The myriad rays that come
From distant galaxies
Bend and cross and sway
As they all arrive
To focus in the eye.

Is a shimmering of light
Less than one of dark?

The Net Folded

It's all there – in the layerings
Dense, wet – heavy,
Dark with smell of ocean,
With seaweed strands still
Braiding sharp scent –

Forming the memory of this day's
Catch – of the waters it went through –

Solidly stowed, waiting, resting,
Readying itself to be picked up;
Lowered once again into the deep –

To catch that which will feed us –
This body, this heart, and this spirit
Each day again.

Talking About Sea

Were I blind like Homer
And yet able to describe the sea
I would be filled with words,
And say

Hear first, then see wave
And rock and pelicans
Heading west into the drowning sun
Drawing the day behind them.

Then say
See the distances
That ships slowly sink into
Turning themselves into memories

I would say
Take the dead
Whose bones are dreams
Whose brains are echoes
In my skull
And whose ears
Will never hear
What my ears hear
And say please

Take the brave prayers,
Of all the ones who ever sailed
And turn them into sails to bring
Safe harbors into view.

I would find a way to sing
To wed the silver and the light –
The salt, the spume, the dark distances
And all the fish
Into one chord.

And then
You would become the sea I sing
And I, your salt

Visible as crystals
Only,
When you turn
And become the air.

Questions

What does the Book say about fathers?
About their sins?

Whose fathers are they?
Did I become a father?
Or the ghost?
Did I invent concerns?
Did I abdicate?
Did I turn away when asked?
Did I fail and smile?
Did I assume the best?
Did I take what wasn't mine?
Did I trust?

And do you love me still?

Enough
To come with me
And be my life?

Pedro Point from Stinson Beach

That cape with its blue gray silhouette
Marks the place the gray whales
Turn in their migrations
East by south
Until they turn again at Palos Verdes
To go straight down to tip of Baja
Where they race home to the nuzzling shallows
In that warm, sheltered, gentle sea
Named for Cortez, to play and love
And sing and calve together.

Then

To return along the well known track
Back up by that very cape
With its blue gray silhouette
Where they sound again heading
Up to the cold pastures

To their other home in that colder
Quadrant of the sea
Without benefit of Bowditch or books
Or implements of any kind.

From here you can see the spouts!

Why am I telling you all this?

Your hands, your hands!

Praises

Sound trumpets – Praise!
Waves roar on the beach in praise –

Each leaf touches the wind
In the forest as it runs through –

The bull bellows – Praise!

There are no fish in the sea
Not playing in water
Praise – Praise – Praise!

The light from the moon praises,
The light from the Sun, from Betelgeuse,
From hearth fire – all Praise –

Roger's drums praise,
Elsa's eyes praise,
The incense praises,
Tamalpais by being, praises,
Roshi Baker praises,
The beach praises.

And the gull at dawn
Skimming the breaking waves
With delight and obedience
To the laws of air
Teaches me too,
To praise.

Saturday Morning

The dolphins pause beyond the breakers
Six of them
Chatting
Being easy with themselves

We see them clearly –

We pause in our walk –
The neighbors come out of their houses
They point –
"So close to the beach" – one says
"In twenty years I've never seen them
     so near" says another
"Are they well? I wonder"
"So beautiful!"

The dark shapes curving into the sea
The morning light
Opening the world

They pause,
They look at us
We see their heads up
Their beaks
Their eyes even

They seem only slightly curious
Before they return to their dancing
Their being easy in the waves.

Three Songs

I: SAILOR'S SONG

Be with me love by the salt sea
With the sound of the bell, be with me.

Be with me love by the hearth's fire
When we're ashore and dry, be with me.

Be with me love in the dawn's light
Before I ship out again, be with me.

Be with me love in the hard storm
When the wind tears, be with me.

Be with me love as I stand watch,
Postponing dreams, be with me.
Be with me love as I wake before dawn
Honing my hopes, be with me.

Be with me love, I give you my soul
And the murmur of doves, be with me.

With the sound of the buoy, be with me.

II: GIRL'S SONG

Necklace, I have a golden necklace,
And when I wear it all the town goes around,
Goes around, goes around,
To see the golden necklace that I wear.

A mandolin, I have a silver mandolin,
And when I play upon its strings
I draw silver music out of air,
And all the men come around
To hear the silver music that I make.

A lake, I have a mist filled lake,
And when I swim within its waters
All the birds come down and fly around
To see splashing of the fish and me.

A heart, I have an aching heart that aches
Because the town, the men, the birds,
And sometimes even I, forget that I am not
The golden necklace nor the mist filled lake,
Nor yet the silver music that I make.

III: BIRD'S SONG

It can be done Lord
Not only Thy will
But mine too

We are unequal partners Lord
But partners still
And I serve you with my life
As you have served me
By giving me my breath,
My soul and will.

Whatever the time Lord
You need me to come or go
Or to witness
Or to mend the pain
I will fly there
And come back again

We are unequal partners Lord
But partners still
And I serve you with my life
As you have served me
By giving me my breath,
My heart and will.

Declaration

I am really getting tired of memorial services.
I am ready to try something else.

Has it been the sense of theater
Required by survivors?

I have had practice
For a lot of years tossing ashes,
My father's and some teachers',
As well as those of a lot of friends.

No one told me I'd grow up to be an ash tosser
And I'd really like to put in
For a different line of work.

Births and marriages
Aren't really my thing anymore
Either
I've done enough of those too.

I'd rather cook for my friends than bury them.

To take up an instrument at my age,
And tone deaf too, won't do.
I'd rather write songs for my friends to sing
And drink and smoke,
And make love and make love,
And make all the stars and planets bring
Their rays
To my love's eyes
In order to inform her
Of the quantity of light
In the universe without which
There would
Have been no life
In the first place
At all.

Recognition

When Alan died I went out to the West Ridge,
Saw sun set in ocean
And heard three new friends
Sit on a Persian carpet I had brought
Sing "Amazing Grace".

When Charles died I went to the office,
Saw sun set in ocean
And the broadcast
Of a convention in Kansas City
Spreading discord.

When my father died I came back home,
Saw no sun rise or set
Heard nothing at all
Knowing I was now on duty
At my world's edge,

And nothing more stood between
Me

And that silence out there.

The Shadow Dance

In Plato's cave we saw the shadows
Dance upon the wall – Today we see
Green figures dance between the ruled
Ledger sheets on which are added
All the dollars spent for this and due for that
Believing the footings to be reality,
Demonstrating worth instead of bone
And sweat and wheat and art
Done for each other in the world.

Spaceborne

for Ruth and Calvin

The trapdoor opened
And down, down
Came the body
Falling, dropping, falling
Down dark
Falling

Snake shedding old skin
Knows

Down
Down through cliff jump,
Down, down, down
Falling, faster, falling
Charms, amulets going
The why, the reasons
All jettisoned
No needs, no shame left

Becoming

By falling
Suddenly clean
Down, down further
Past gravity's hold
Past the planet
Out free
Into the dark
No longer falling

Space borne

Seeing

No longer falling

Being.

Varda Poem

For Yanko

You who taught numbers to know the rainbow,
Who opened the gates to the celestial city
Who always made more when there was less
Who enchanted the birds
Who loved all things except the mean
Should you be seen
Dancing in your golden ashes
About half a league off our port beam
As we go out the Gate
While the sun sets clear
Will you tell us one more time
How hard it is to be human
When it's so easy to be divine.

Day on the Bay

The wind comes, the wind goes
Full sun, felucca sail,
Bright red, yellow, blue,
White foam, grey green seas,
The perfume of young eyes
Discovering the world.

Wrinkles and laughter at the tiller.
Leather, salt, wood –

The sound of a flute when
The wind rests at dusk
The first stars bobbing on the outgoing tide.

Oedipus, Ariadne, Sappho will be born
Soon – or is it long ago they died?

Offshore winds –
The perfume of young eyes.

Address to the Singer

There – the flame burns clearly –
The incense echoes the fragrance of forests and
Musk of memory is in the evening air.

The hollyhocks, the cosmos,
Violet flowers, pale in the dusk
The late jacaranda blooming
As the sea turns itself into darkness.

I have not yet learned to speak
To the dead, nor to hear them
When they speak to me which is why
I address you Irenei, who are here –
Expression of the same heart
Beating in Toni's breast until
This late last early spring.

This day the sun sets, tomorrow
The days that are left to us will begin
Once again to drift down into the sand.

Irenei! Where is she now, your sister,
Our friend, the one who brought you?
You! Irenei! voice of her heart
Tell us how she is –

This violet evening
This midsummer dusk –

For Toni

When breath and soul have done
With body's use
And heart and mind are free at last
To soar into eternal light
The lessons learned and taught
Are burned to ashes for an instant
Before joining once again into the dance.

The dance begins
With seed and flower
Which turns to fruit and tree
And then into the music
Making for
The bell's sound, the stomp,
The thunder, cicada's whirring,
Bird talk, the dolphin's click
The whale's song –
The wind, all surrounded
By the splash of water.

We are all joined
By the marvel of our being,
The essence of our consciousness,
The measure of our strengths

And by the sense of having been
Part of Toni's life – and now –
Addressing that other fraction
All ash and crystal
We put to rest in good earth
Surrounded by seed, flowers,
Fruit, trees and smoke –
The memory endures
While the dance begins again!

For the Person Who Sounds the Future

You arrive like lightning dragging
    your thunder made of a jacket of fur
    across this pavement of gray clouds –

You who arrive like a leopard coming out
    of the dark silence of the jungle
    tearing the moment with your teeth
    made of pearls –

You who arrive like a warrior dressed
    in light vaulting over unforgettable
    obstacles to grasp the present made
    of silver wares –

You who arrive like a smile shooting
    the arrows of the future with your
    rainbow created in weathers more
    gentle and blue

You who arrive in brilliance – while I go
    to find flags, sounds, flowers,
    rhythms, winds, landscapes, rocks,
    mountains, lagoons and breakers like
    the horses of the sea whose manes
    are made of joy – for you

To celebrate your arrival!

For Love That's Given

When payment of any kind
Is expected by the giver,
It is not love that's given –

Seed planted in receiving earth
Gives all to stalk of wheat,
Apple tree or fir
Without regret –
It gives, and giving all
Fulfills its role.

Ask no return
Of child, of lover
Or even of the busy world.

It comes
When it's not asked, as wind comes,
Or rain, unexpectedly,

And then
Comes back again,
Again.

Henrietta

This is for you
While the grass grows green
In this full spring moon
And the gentle wind
Touches you in those far places

This is for you
While the cherry tree blossoms
In the fine light air
And the rose light
Touches you in those far places

This is for you
While the tide runs out
To the sea's embraces
And my mind's eye
Touches you in those far places

Steel Striding

for Mark

Steel striding across this land!

Exuberant calligraphy
Accumulating delight for all of us
Its thrust the affirmation
That steel can –
That man can –
That joy can –
All converge simultaneously
Into an expression that moves
Gently beyond all the givens,
The acceptable, the reasonable,
And the traditional.

You are the child still,
In clarity,

You say "Honor the Treaties"
You say
"Don't be good, be great"
You say "Do it"
And you do, with steel.

Your crane sings!
Your torch sings!
Your truck sings!
Your cables sing!

And your pieces stand
Full of space
Striding across this land!

Go Daughter of Mine

Go daughter of mine
Into the valleys and harbors
Knowing that richness is there
And that all is as possible
As nothing –
It's merely a matter of choice.

    Sweet are the apples of London
    With your true love waiting
    And remember that daughters of sailors
    Keep an eye on the wind.

Go daughter of mine
Into the learning
Knowing that sorrow is there
In spite of the giving and growing
And that
It's always a matter of choice.

    Curved are the ways of the world
    With one life waiting
    And remember that daughters of sailors
    Keep an eye on the wind.

Go daughter of mine
Into this age and universe
Knowing the old dreams work
And that it's not only a matter
Of music
It's also a matter of choice

    Your courage is grist for the journey
    Your art, the art of the possible
    And remember that daughters of sailors
    Keep an eye on the wind.

For the Marriage of Romana & Nico

They climbed the stairs that day
The two of them,
Looking for all the world to see,
As if all the angels had come down
To touch them with delicate glances
And flutters of golden feathers.

All the clouds 'round the rainbow
Turned into flowers that day!

Then they went into the house
At the top of the stairs
Together that day
In a way they had never been before!

And later,
When they came out to look –

The world had changed –

The bud had turned into flower
The future assumed its shape,

And the dancing really began
For love and for each other!

That Which Is

Staggering, sleepless and unsteady
Our progress towards the stars is not perceptible
We redo the twenty million years
Since we crawled out of the briny in nine months.
Each time I've had a child, all of it again.
Not having learned it by myself
But out of the old knowledge of the blood.

Our understanding of the universe has changed
Since my father's day.
His first command
A sailing ship in the Red Sea,
While my son could live to ride
A shuttle between the stars.
And yet
I have no faith in the good outcome of the journey.
Hope yes,
As the sun rises
And the sea rolls –
I am concerned
About how we are
Each to each,
As we go along the way –

The new born harp seal clubbed to death
Does not demand respect. It deserves,
As all living things deserve –
As the bag woman, the gimp,
The blind and even your enemy deserve.

We are all manifestations of the light.

The food chains begin with light
The mind in the waters feeds on light
We grow, move, touch and love
Always reaching for the light.
We give many names to it.

There have been experts of the light, guardians.
Regenerators, priests, housekeepers
Chemists, dealers and obfuscators;
Without it
No Bodhi Tree, no St. John of the Cross.

When we die we go back into it.

The light.

Progress

Eighty thousand years ago
The language that we had was made of grunts
And yowls and laughs; and bones
And clubs served as the entire arsenal for all of us.

Today the description of a rose knows a hundred
Thousand ways to be – while the sophistication
Of the armaments we have has grown commensurately.

If we can learn to use our words to stave off
The destruction of all that we've become
We will have taken a stride across the ground
In which we've buried ancestors –

While we still grunt and yowl and laugh
And scream in bed knowing how joyous
It is to be alive today.

It Did Not Start Hesitantly

It did not start hesitantly.
There was no question
At the beginning.
The questions came later
On the way to Hawaii,
In the hotel room in London.
While planning the trip to Vallarta,
The one to Venice not taken;

During the ones in front of the fire
At the beach, in the mountains.

It became no longer a question
Of questions, it became blame,
Unfilled glasses, not enough
Of what there was –
Though it was more than
Either one of us had dreamt.

It did not start diffidently.
There was a subtle certainty that led
Us from plant to flower and
From rug to dawn to edge
Of precipice and back –
Your father's faithlessness
And my mother's power
Were cut up and put back together
In assorted envelopes.
Territories were staked, and
Treaties made in earnest
To cover the land as the rivers ran.

Proof, continuous proof,
Velvet rope of proof, star,
Ship of proof, house roofed
With it, bids made of it,

Teasing of it,
Reaching for it –
Proof!

And there is none now
Except the one that we are here
As at the start, not hesitant,
As at the start, not diffident,
Now stripping all
So that at last
Our bones touch

And there is no question left
Between.

Corollary

That which wakes us to move
Out in the morning
And back again at night
Is the same force
That moves the tides.

We believe we have invented.
All the reasons for all things.

The wisdom implicit in the bed
And what we go there for
Is perhaps greater
Than all that taught
In the universities.

Garland

for CJ

I

I wait for your body, lithe like that of
    a girl, to come running
Up the stairs to me who have been waiting
    for you to return from your visit
To a strange land of a different kind
    of love with your new lover
While I have been busy exploring the
    byways of my own doings.

I wait for your smile to rise above
    the corner of the balustrade
That kept us from falling in
    the days when we were
Arranging this house and changing
    it from your place to our place
While we, bundling our separate
    pasts into closets and boxes, smiled.

I wait for your heart which has
    waited too long now
Knowing that when the rose blooms
    the petals never go back
Into the folds of the bud from
    which they came
While the wind sends the perfume
    of your life into air.

II

You, beautiful as you are
Have become other

Now no longer
What you were

With me when we met
And the rivers merged

All during the years
Solstice and equinox, dawns,
Stars and sunsets became ours.
You, though other
Are part of me still,

As you move away
Down the corridor of your life.
You leave me wondering whether
When we touch again
Your violet heart will know me
And whether that other part of me
Which is you, still will be beautiful
As you are.

III

It's what we do with it
After we've gotten up one day
And discovered for the first time
That the quantity of days remaining
Is measurable.

One can and does get to a point
Where the bottom of the jar
Is visible

And then
If one does not turn,

Then one will not become
The violet presence
The heron's flight
The crocus' blossoms
One would stay there

Picking agates up
On the near shore, happily enough
Watching stars surrender light
While vaguely remembering
There was to have been
Another thing.

IV

It comes on in bouts,
At certain times and hours
As some migraines
Or even as some mini seasons
Of the soul.

During the morning shower
While brushing teeth or dressing.
During the walk downstairs,
The drive to the office;
When the telephone rings –

While glancing at certain books
While seeing clearly or not; with or without
Glasses or reason, the pieces
Of the time together –
The marble table at Enrico's,
And a certain gray blue look that
Embraces and impales at the same instant,

It feels as if the hammer of my heart
Drives all good and loving sense
Out of my blood which runs out
Arteries, up veins, through flesh, all of
Which were made by you

All busy screaming your name.

V

Heart beats
Slow
All
Is
Out there
Waiting
We are here
Don't know
What will come
Or become of us

You say
I am free
I shrug
Not knowing I was bound

I have my heart
In my hands now

You go
Bird wing beating
I know
Please go.

VI

Now no more
No more
You have taken
All that was
Together
Now no more

The full moon barks
And it's finished
And you will not touch me
Any more.

VII

The storm recedes
The beams creak
Settling back into place
The sand stipples the window glass
And my bones are cold
Even though a small fire burns

I go from room to room
Padding like an old caged lion
Hunting your spoor here and there
As if we were still in the plains
Below the mountains in the tall grass
When I would catch you by the neck

And you'd growl and roar
And a flock of finches
Would wheel in the dark blue sky
While the tall grass lay flat
Where we had been.

The cold is in my bones
And I go back and forth
And back and forth
While the small fire burns
And the storm recedes.

VIII

Without a keel
Our sloop could never reach
Ports we both desired.

Now its bones are beached
In winter surf.
The full moon's tide is up.
The waves keep coming in.

They're called breakers
For the reason that they are.

I look at the splintered wreckage
The snapped mast, the sheets all tangled,
The canvas torn, the hull stove in,
A ripped cushion from the saloon,
The galley's pieces, the bunks,
The bright work in the sand,
And see only our sloop scudding
Before the wind, seeming sound
Enough for us and for all to see;

Incapable, however, of tacking
Up into the wind and harbor
When the storm did come.

IX

Now it's truly over, the tide is down,
Most of the garden's gone to sea
And what's left is battered and undone
With bands of junk and sea grass marking
The new places where the surf reached up
To tear and wound and cleanse
This coast this last time round.

"It's never been as rough as this," they say.

I now watch the waves breaking on the sand
Seeing in a way I never saw before
The torn and jagged shape of this land's edge.
And the promenade of strangers on the beach.

It is all new and rough, but new it is;
Even the sea's reflection in the house is new.

I now see that this sea I watch
Sees me as well as you across itself

I feel it wonders what we'll do with it
When you come back to find it new,
Strange, perhaps, and torn, but sound.

Oh, let us dance it differently
This coming time around!

          X

And you came back
Full of gifts and grace, wanting still
To know that everything was new.

I was glad
To hold you in my arms,
And begged you to finish it with him,
To come back easy
And to come with me,
With me, for us.

It was your head
That brought you back –

Your heart had changed,
And your body found a different way to be.

Poetry works,
Perhaps,
But only for a while.
Dishes were still there to do
And petals will not fold
Back into the buds they were.

Petals turn and smile and fall
While I go back to park the car

And through the motions of my day
Knowing, though all is not the same,
We met for each other's good,
And that there is change, not blame.

You are your future

And your heart
Is changed.

XI

Yes,
It is Spring.
The cymbidium is in bloom,
The pelargonium everywhere
And the daisies are all smiles.

The gulls wheel in the sun
And the wheel goes round.

At sun set I give thanks,
And my wishes for our lives.

XII

The dusk is gone,
The night is long
And full of waking.

This time there is nothing to be said
And there is no word
Left
In the silence of my heart.

The Grey Heron in the Garden

It is the curve of your neck that I saw.

With a child's eye
At Yamanaka
When I discovered the color green
In the pine woods
And the smell of blue smoke
At dusk.

Then at Karuisawa
Before going up
Into the Alps on that trip
Walking
Into the petrified forest
At dawn.

Yesterday, after lunch
In the garden
Beyond the pines I planted
On this side of the ocean
Into a sky made of grey pearl
You rose to fly.

It is the curve of your neck that I saw.

Hang Gliders

We rush to this ridge
Or wind up the mountain
To find the wind of the spirit
That will lift our hearts
Into the air.

We build delicate sails
To mimic hawks and gulls
To get us off
To raise our bodies high
Into the air.

But first we must be well placed
With our houses in order
And the heart fair
And then look –
Look, there, there!

Harmony

In order to sustain the order of all things,
To bring into the universe of self the song
Of the eternal, one learns and sings
The song of Shiva's magic drum along

The byways of creation until the letters
Of the Word become flesh, become desire,
For then the dance continues without fetters –
As movement fulfilled in and of itself, in fire,

In wind, in moving clouds, in dancing leaves
And all the other manifestations of the power
Which shapes our consciousness and grieves
When we are separate, alone as a single flower.

In this Kalpa, the power of the dove
Is even greater than the Eagle's: it is of love.

Every Thing

For Barbara

Every thing –
Each and every sun set
Sun rise, rain fall, cloud
Shadow, leaf and heart
Beat that brought
Us now to this place
This time in the clear
Sense of our being
I give thanks
To
And
Dance now
And am made more
Than I was by being
Aware of your hand's touch
Your eyes' look and
More than lemon grass or
Pelargonium infuse my life's
Brew with the sense of who
We are together
When we are
Every
Thing.

The Promised Land

They were full of themselves, the Ostrogoths,

Having climbed the mountain passes,
Outflanked the cold's edge with their own steel
They paused above the green plains.

They looked south towards the sun

Marvelling at the richness, knowing
The long valleys, the orchards and flocks
To have been readied for them.

Taller and lighter far than the squat serfs
Hunched and laboring in the fields
The children of the Sun were coming home.

Those bred out Romans
Rotten with pleasure
Bursting like pomegranates when touched
Had had it all too long.

This was the land where oranges
Blossom in the spring and doves
Whirr and nights are soft.

They never thought themselves conquerors –
They knew themselves to be
Barbaric, strange, cruel even,
But this was their land,

And they were coming home!

Prismatic Function

The marriage of dissimilars
Unifies the world
Love itself becomes
The bridge builder.

Clear almond eyes
Framed in cocoa skin –
Viking mane a halo for
The Mediterranean face –
A German learns Swahili

Difficulties of travel in the past
Made for inbreeding –
The marriage of cousins!
Too much of that –
You see what happens to dogs,
Splayed hips, bad backs.

The village is global!
Rainbow in the playground!
My brother in the antipodes!

Nephews send me news
Of distances that are next door –
My daughter in a garden
In England sends a Chinese card –

The language we speak
Is human.

Eight Views of the World

for Satty

ONE

In the center of the Universe
There is a Hole

That Hole is filled with Palaces
And Grace and Courtyards
And the Jewel in its Middle

But Word's gotten out
That the Hole can now be reached
And expeditions of all kinds have been mounted
To get Man there
Astronauts vying with mystics
To be first

In a corner of the Hole
Field mice are busy nibbling
Making it
LARGER

TWO

All the world's roses on a raft
Carmen's rose and the last rose,
The rose of Agincourt and the rose of China
Rosemary and rosebud and rosebush
Rose of Sharon, tea rose and Rosalind
A rafting of roses down the dark river

Pay attention nobly born
Pay attention now that time has come
Absolute roseate time
Not the quarter hour or the five after
Or the ten before
But time itself
To take you as a child again
Into its moonscaped mountains

THREE

First light
Then fire
Then filament of fire
Then suddenly
Stone
Your eyes
Till the Universe
With Noise and Clanging
Each time

This happens each time
A star explodes
This happens each time
A child is born

FOUR

Your great horned head
Rules your kingdom with divine grace
The essential Empress
Containing
Appetites and children,
Devouring Satan, and the wind –

Roses lie spilled at your feet –
Islands spewing fire
Burn steadily behind your walls of water –
The heart's lyre reverberates –

The rocks are symbols of your majesty
Your gray cat its guardian

I stare and see myself

There is all tenderness
And no forgiveness
In your glance –
You too remember the labyrinth

FIVE

"Oh my God!" said James to Cock Robin
As they sat under the lip
Of the iceberg whiskery with froth
"Is that your tiny heart at last
"Fluttering its way out into the world?"

"Now we can be together truly
"We're perfect you and I
"On the threshold of galaxies
"And no monsters will dare
"Bother us ever again."

"The water keeps on flowing.
"Where does it go?" said Cock Robin

SIX

Hey what would you do
If you were me
And had caught the terrible
Beast of Blee

Would you laugh and wonder
And ring a bell
Or clutch your bowels
And run like hell

Would you leave your mother
On a sandy shore
Playing guitar
And pulling an oar.

Now if you had caught
The Beast of Blee
I'd come to help you
And you'd be me!

SEVEN

Each bird attached to
And supported by its own column of air
Moves through skies of clouds
Weaving its way into eternity

A grandmother will play
Through a child's hands
Sets the jewel firmly on the brow
And protects

The landscape of awareness
Is filled with birds
Weaving their columns
In and out

Around the bend
There is a great light

EIGHT

"With dreams upon my bed" said Blake
"Thou scarest and affrightest me".
He said

At the end of the night
For that ride in the dark
To the laddering window's lip
To the rat's nest and the hanged man
And the dreadful dark of the sea

Face to face with the face of God
Knowing not if it be
A dream of birth or a dream of death
Or a dream of the terrible sea

"With Visions"
He said

Invocation

Greater than the Yang Tze Kiang
Greater than the four mighty rivers
        in the fountain in the Piazza Navona
The Nile, the Ganges, the Amazon and
        the dark gray Danube.
Greater than all but the river of time itself
You timeless one,
Great river of money
Flow incessantly
Across
Our geographies.

As the earth turns you move
Draining, collecting, eroding,
Tearing, flooding, drowning
And empowering your people.

Silent, green river,
Stored behind dams,
Secure within your banks,
Charger of turbines,
Destroyer and builder –
Haven for birds,
For fish of the rapids,
Carrier of vessels –
Feeder of gardens –
No crops become harvest,
No grain is stored
No abundance smiles
Without you.

River of power, of appetites
Teacher and master
Creature of Kali
Despot
You

To whom too many
Have pledged allegiance
River of Baal
Great green river of money
Creature of Kali
Despot
You.

Become servant
That the light
Be served.

Gauguin's Self Portrait

It was not the former banker's eye
Tired of grey Parisian boulevards
That had dreamt of far away colors
And an unshackled life –
That looked out at us.

It was the direct eye of one who had fought
To find his place on the planet –

He looked at us saying,

"But then, I took the chance,
"To work it out,

"To be – and here I am."

Road Poem

To save the soul
The body suffers so much!

All the Jihads, the Holy Wars,
The Massacres – St. Bartholomew's
The Golden Temple, Tehuantepec,
Auschwitz, Bergen-Belsen, the Inquisition,
Athletes in Munich! Soweto!
The Ardeatine caves!

Now airplanes blow out of the sky!
All for someone's hope of Heaven!
At the same time
The nurturing of life
Goes on
The gardeners, the nurses!

Somehow gentleness prevails
Even as the fires rage –

The seamlessness of water!

I sit by the road's edge
Fascinated by the power
Of a new green leaf
Forcing its way up
Through the gravel, the concrete –
Through the layering of civilization
Into the light.

Alarms

The house is on fire!
The tiger's in the yard!

The tools have run away with our future!
Alarms! Alarms!

The lion and the lamb,
The falcon and the patriot,
The banker, the chief, the priest,
The renegade and child
Yes, all of us

As the singer says,
Must come together
Willingly
To be together
In the light

As, never, never before

Now.

Measure

To have known the splendor of the rose,
Worked through a storm at sea,
Delighted in a smile at dawn
And tasted of the grace of God
Is measure of a life.

To have helped others
To the same feast
Is that by which
Other lives are measured.

Stuff

The large rock
At the end of the spit
Resonates with a slower beat
Than the wave.

•

It is difficult
To cut the air
With straight lines.

•

One cannot force the door
To be more open than open.

•

"There are only two things I hate,"
The cowboy said,
"And both are losing."

•

First light,
Seen only by wastrels and workers.

•

Birds dive to catch fish,
Fish fly to avoid being eaten.

•

The same air carries
Both hawk and pigeon.

•

Religion is no substitute for wings.

•

First in the race, last in the fields.

•

Buy when the streets are running blood,
Sell when the orchard is in flower.

•

The hand that reaches for the light touch
May be great on an axehandle.

•

Hedge your bets, but bet your ass.

•

Write for that feeling of delight
As others dance,
And others make their music,
And others plant and pot,
But write.

•

The barking dog announces the philosopher.

•

Even when the jug is upside down
Water will run down hill.

•

There are no things about which
It's better not to think too much.

•

In the guise of a man
Leaving a farmyard
Looking up at the forest ridge
Pan
Said
"I've always had a thing for goats."

•

If one does not lie down with laughter,
One wakes with tears.

•

Poetry –
Spend a minute –

This is the place the land stops.
Houses along the beach are quiet,

It is so quiet
I hear the snails calling,
Crawling, on the window glass.

Wishes like the stars
Help us set our course.

So many ways the sea comes
To touch the land
Riding and roaring on the rising beach
Breaking on rocks,
Gliding into lagoons,
Lapping up against man made docks,
Each time reminding us
Of the last time it took possession
When the Milky Way banded
The sky from South to North

•

Our fears brilliant and visible
In the dark,
Shining like buoys, like lighthouses
Like bobbing salmon boats
Attracting us and warning us away.

•

The infinite ability to renew hope
Runs through our kind.

•

Of one mind with Shakespeare
Marlowe, Patchen, Thomas,
And Rexroth who still speak
For all of us –
And make us face the page
To see the glory and malice
Threaded through its fabric

•

Not Dream

It came out of the kiva
And danced that night –
Naked but for the deer belt;

Became the buck, startled,
Chased through brush
Reaching the high prairie –
Hooves drumming, going,
The sound sustaining it,
Air rushing, going, getting away,
Down by the river
Through the cottonwoods;
More trail, more scent
More piñon,
Back up to the mesa
Hooves drumming
Going, going
Through the piñon
Fast, going,
Lungs heaving,
Stopping finally
Alone under the stars;
Lungs heaving,
Pink foam at the nostrils –

Great gasps
Devouring the air
Trembling
Legs twitching,
Standing, twitching,
Stopping, waiting,

Until after one huge breath
My heart suddenly
Slowed
And walked back to the house
And knew where it had been.

And we held each other
Until day broke.

There are Certain Goodbyes

English goodbyes, lover's goodbyes,
Goodbyes gladly given and taken,
Frantic goodbyes, hopeless ones –
Ones that are torn out of eyes that will never see
Goodbyes that are mute, silent acknowledgments –
Goodbyes that are kind,
Goodbyes made of leather, for long roads –
Goodbyes filled with prayers and candles,
Dutiful goodbyes that always taste of mint,
Familial goodbyes made of noise,
       of rainbows, of food and of wine
Goodbyes made of vast silences, the Mongol's eye
       and distances –
Muffled goodbyes, made of death breath,
       of splayed hope against hope
       and of the spirit almost triumphant –

The child's goodbye, saucy, worldly and eager
The goodbye one gives one's self when
       the walking papers come,
The headmaster's goodbye to the students,
The goodbye of dawn reserved
       for pilgrims and soldiers;
The shouted goodbye drifting over wave spume,
       caught in the winds, blown
       back to shore, echoing –

Goodbyes that are not leavetakings, nor
       even farewells but open parentheses,
Sour, reproachful goodbyes, genial ones –
The painful ones, made of torn flesh, because
       there is never enough time, place or understanding;
The goodbye for enemies.

Goodbyes reserved for strangers met on trains –
Goodbyes constructed for statues, for dolls, for stuffed animals.

Goodbyes that sting, that never look back,
          that are left on pieces of paper,
Others that jostle and even stumble,
That are brave and jocular or made of jade

All the world's goodbyes

And this one is mine
And this one is yours.

Farewell to the House of These Years

To leave a house
In which love lives
Is as difficult as being born –
With no knowledge
Once again
Of that which waits outside.

Where is all the furniture to go?
Where the pictures of the children,
And Nonna Anna's crystal bowl?

That painting and those books,
And Alfonso's piper on the mantelpiece,
The rugs full of laughter,
Where?

It's also learning how to die
Once more
Leaving all behind –
Again like being born –
About to be freed and bound again
As much by need
As by having wanted a thing too much
Now – and not again.